ROBERT JOHNSON
for Ukulele

Arranged by Pete Billmann

Robert Johnson photo booth self portrait, early 1930s
© 1986 Delta Haze Corporation
All Rights Reserved Used by Permission

ISBN 978-1-4584-5965-7

HAL•LEONARD®
CORPORATION

7777 W. BLUEMOUND RD. P.O. BOX 13819 MILWAUKEE, WI 53213

Visit Hal Leonard Online at
www.halleonard.com

Dead Shrimp Blues

Words and Music by Robert Johnson

*Chord symbols reflect basic harmony.

I've served my best bait, ba - by, _____ and I can't do that no harm. _____

𝄋 Verse

3. Ev - 'ry - thing ___ I do, babe, you got your
5. Now you tak - en my shrimp, ba - by, _____ you

mouth ___ stuck out. _____ Hole where I used to fish, ___ you got me post - ed out. ___ Ev - 'ry - thing
know you turned me down. I could - n't do noth - in' un - til I got my - self un - wound. You _____

1st time, w/ Rhy. Fig. 1
2nd time, w/ Rhy. Fig. 1 (1st 6 meas.)

I do, _____ you got your mouth stuck out.
tak - en my ___ shrimp, ___ oo, _____ know you turned ___ me down. ___

To Coda ⊕

At the hole where I used to fish, ___ ba - by, ___ you got me post - ed out. ___
Babe, I could - n't do noth - in' ___ un - til I got my - self un - wound. ___

4

Drunken Hearted Man

Words and Music by Robert Johnson

*Chord symbols reflect basic harmony.

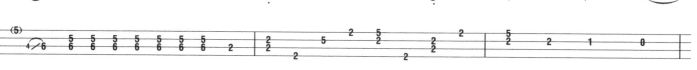

my way of liv-in', ___ it would mean so much __ to me. ___

Verse

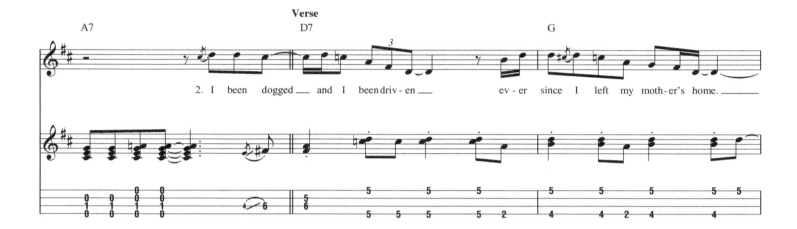

2. I been dogged __ and I been driv-en __ ev-er since I left my moth-er's home. ___

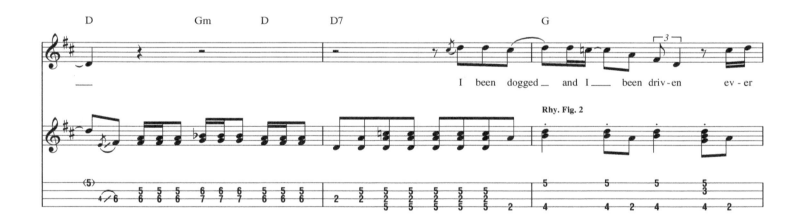

I been dogged __ and I __ been driv-en ev-er

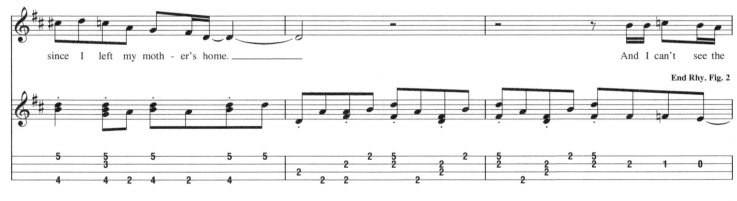

since I left my moth-er's home. _____ And I can't see the

w/ Rhy. Fig. 1

rea - son why _____ that I can't leave these no - good wom - ens a - lone. _____

Verse

3. My fa - ther died and left me, _____ my poor moth - er done _ the best that she could. _____

My

w/ Rhy. Fig. 2 (1st 3 meas.)

fa - ther died _ and left me, my poor ma - ma done the best _____ she could. _

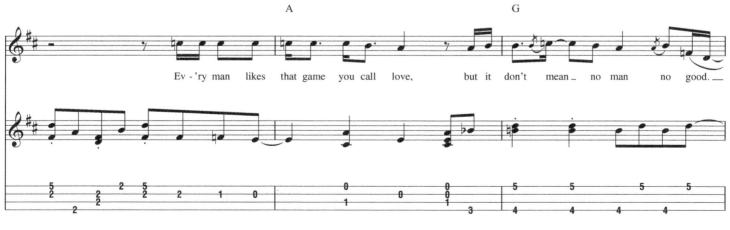

Ev - 'ry man likes that game you call love, but it don't mean _ no man no good. _

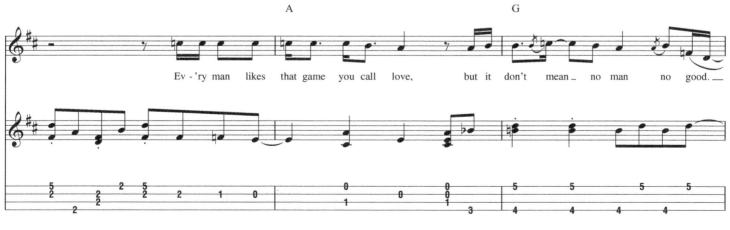

4. Now, I'm the drunk - en heart - ed man ___ and

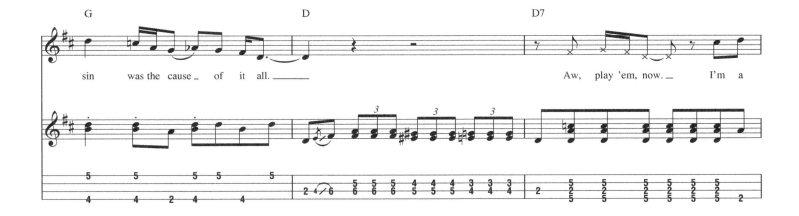

sin was the cause ___ of it all. ___ Aw, play 'em, now. ___ I'm a

w/ Rhy. Fig. 2

drunk-en heart - ed man and sin was the cause of it all. ___ And the day that you

w/ Rhy. Fig. 1

get weak for no - good wom-en, that's the day that you bound to fall. ___

From Four Until Late

Words and Music by Robert Johnson

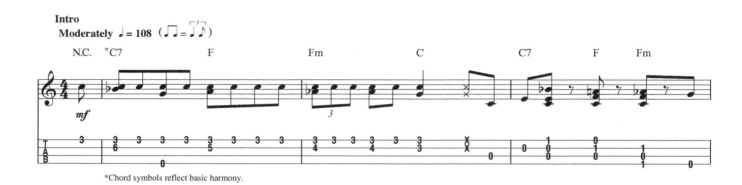

*Chord symbols reflect basic harmony.

1. From four ___ un - til late, I was wring - in' my hands ___ and cry'n'. ___
   phis to Nor - folk is a thir - ty - six hours' _____ ride. ___
3., 4., 5. *See additional lyrics*

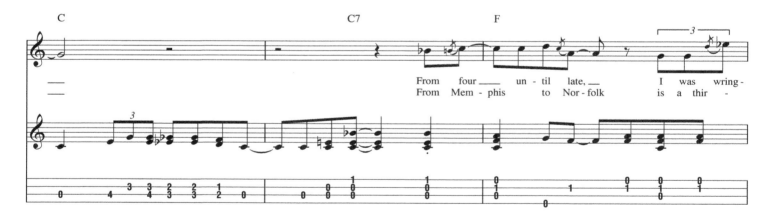

From four ___ un - til late, ___ I was wring -
From Mem - phis to Nor - folk is a thir -

in' my hands ___ and cry'n'. ___ I be - lieve
ty - six hours' _____ ride. ___ A man is

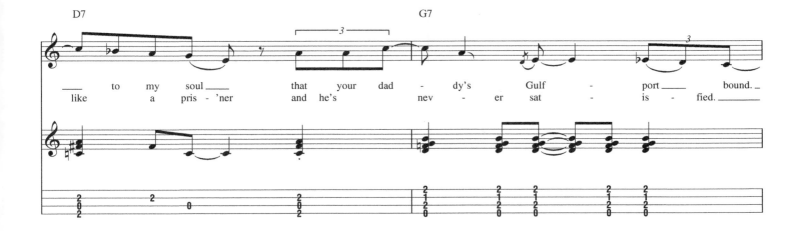

_____ to my soul _____ that your dad - dy's Gulf - port _____ bound. _
like a pris - 'ner and he's nev - er sat - is - fied. _____

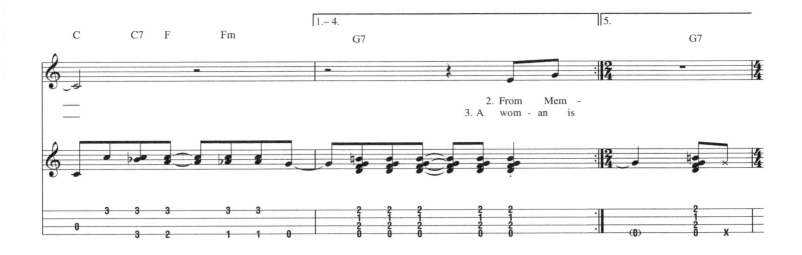

2. From Mem -
3. A wom - an is

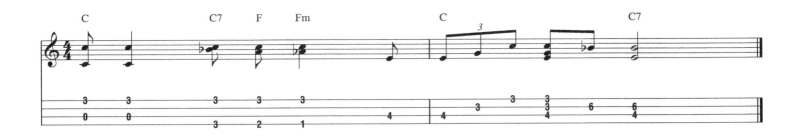

Additional Lyrics

3. A woman is like a dresser,
   Some man always ramblin' through its drawers.
   A woman is like a dresser,
   Some man's always ramblin' through its drawers.
   It cause so many men wear an apron overhall.

4. From four until late,
   She get with a no-good bunch and clown.
   From four until late,
   She get with a no-good bunch and clown.
   Now she won't do nothin'
   But tear a good man reputation down.

5. When I leave this town,
   I'm 'on' bid you fare, farewell.
   And when I leave this town,
   I'm gon' bid you fare, farewell.
   And when I return again,
   You'll have a great long story to tell.

Honeymoon Blues

Words and Music by Robert Johnson

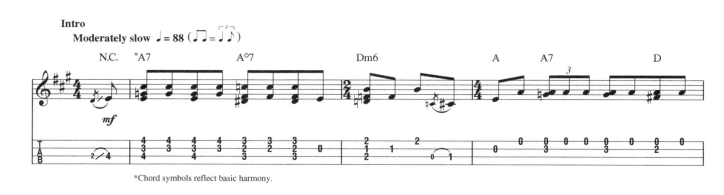

*Chord symbols reflect basic harmony.

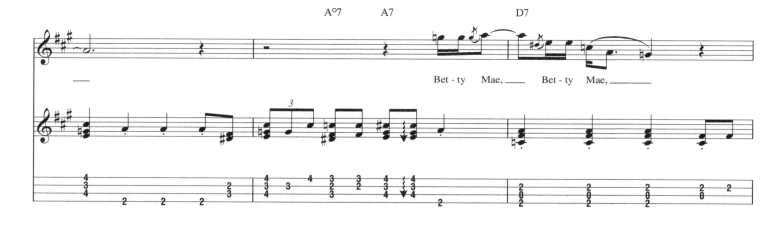

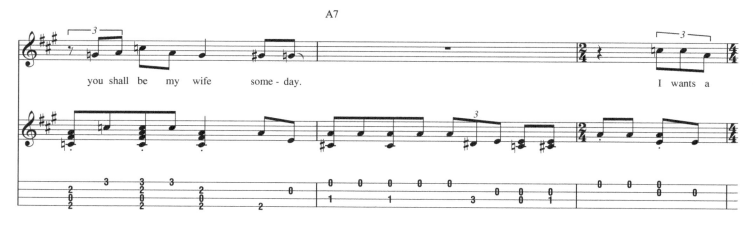

lit - tle sweet girl _____ that will do an - y - thing ____ that I say. _____

Verse

2. Bet - ty Mae, you is my heart - string. ____ You is my ____ des - ti - ny.

End Rhy. Fig. 1

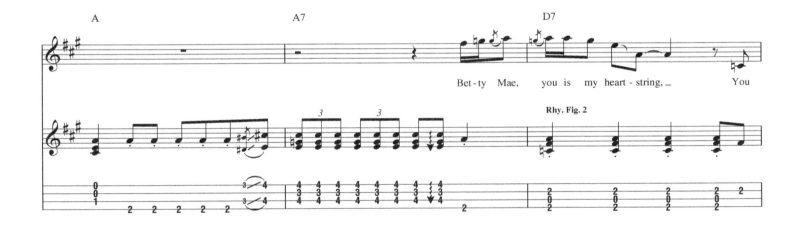

Bet - ty Mae, you is my heart - string, ____ You

Rhy. Fig. 2

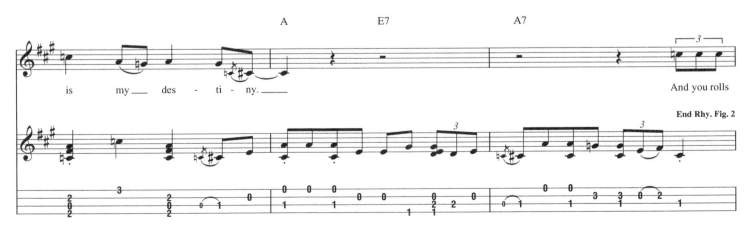

is my ____ des - ti - ny. _____

And you rolls

End Rhy. Fig. 2

13

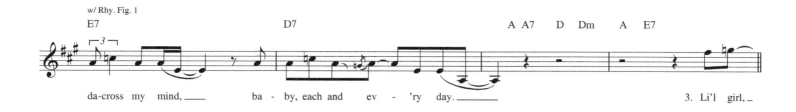

da-cross my mind, ____ ba - by, each and ev - 'ry day. ____ 3. Li'l girl, __

Verse

__ li'l girl, ____ my life __ seem so mis - er - y. ____ Mm, mm, __

__ lit - tle girl, ____ my life seem so mis - er - y. ____

Ba - by, I guess it must be love, now, __ hmm, __

__ Lord, __ that's tak - in' ef - fect on me. ____ 4. Some - day I

Verse

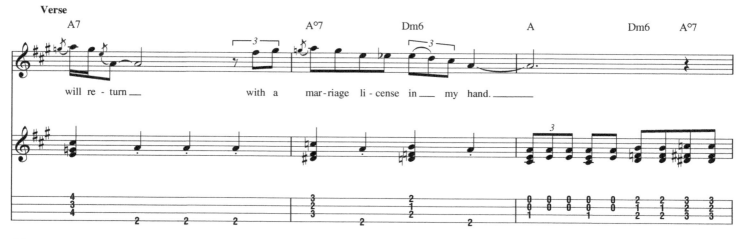

will re - turn __ with a mar - riage li - cense in __ my hand. ____

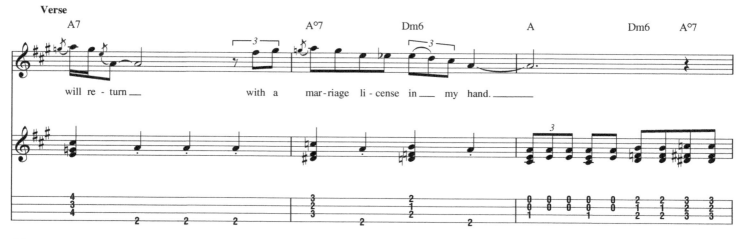

14

I Believe I'll Dust My Broom

Words and Music by Robert Johnson

*Chord symbols reflect basic harmony.

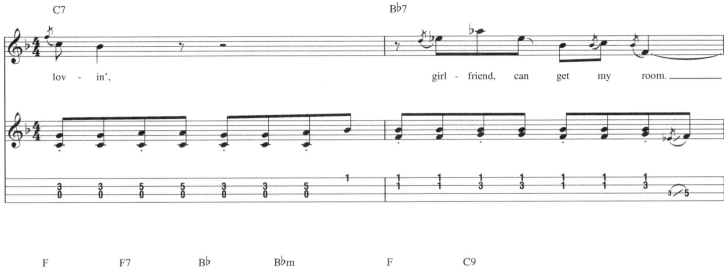

lov - in',   girl - friend, can get my room. _____

2. I'm gon'

write a let - ter,
want no wom - an _____ wants ev-'ry down - town ___ man ___ she meet. ___   tel - e - phone ___
5., 6. *See additional lyrics*

___ ev-'ry town I know.   I'm gon' write a let - ter,
I don't want no wom - an _____ wants ev-'ry

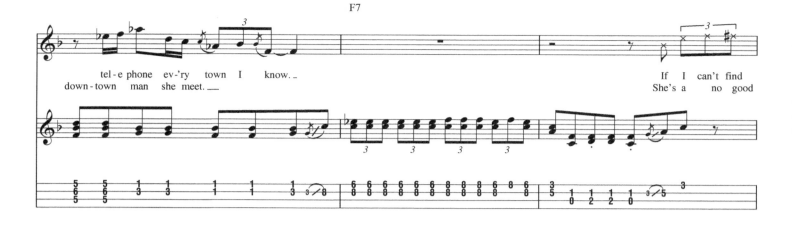

tel - e phone ev - 'ry town I know. ___
down - town man she meet. ___

If I can't find
She's a no good

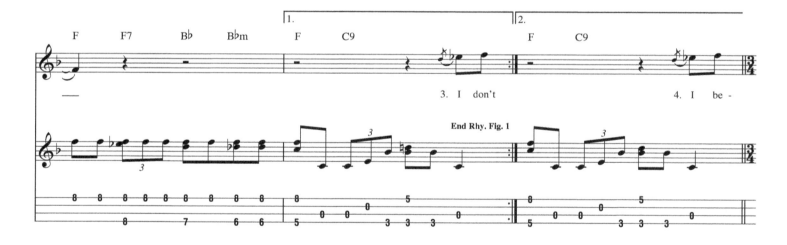

To Coda ⊕

her in West Hel-'na,
don - ey, ___

she must be in East Mon - roe, I know. ___
they should-n't al - low her on the street.

—

3. I don't

4. I be -

End Rhy. Fig. 1

Verse

lieve, ___

I be - lieve ___ I'll go

Additional Lyrics

5. And I'm gettin' up in the mornin',
   I believe I'll dust my broom.
   I'm gettin' up in the mornin',
   I believe I'll dust my broom.
   Girlfriend, the black man you been lovin',
   Girlfriend, can get my room.

6. I'm gon' call up Chiney,
   See is my good girl over there.
   I'm gon' call up China,
   See is my good girl over there.
   If I can't find her on Phillipine's Island,
   She must be in Ethiopia somewhere.

I'm a Steady Rollin' Man

(Steady Rollin' Man)

Words and Music by Robert Johnson

*Chord symbols reflect basic harmony.

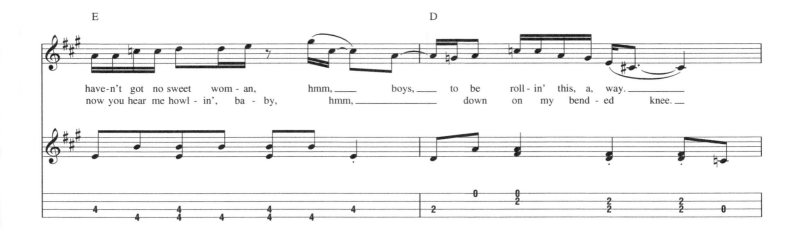

have-n't got no sweet wom-an, hmm, ____ boys, ____ to be roll-in' this, a, way. ____
now you hear me howl-in', ba-by, hmm, _____ down on my bend-ed knee. __

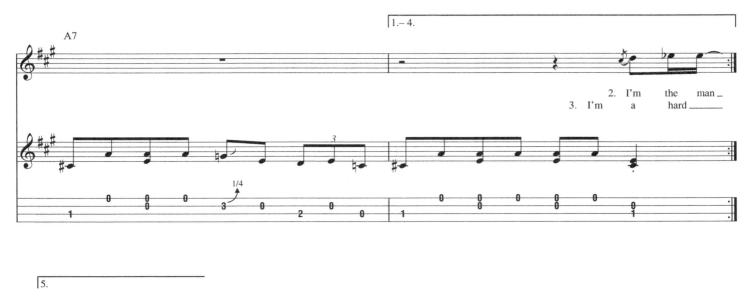

2. I'm the man __
3. I'm a hard _____

Additional Lyrics

3. I'm a hard workin' man,
   Have been for many years, I know.
   I'm a hard workin' man,
   Have been for many long years, I know.
   And some cream puff's usin' my money,
   Oo, well, babe, but that'll never be no more.

4. You can't give your sweet woman
   Everything she wants in one time.
   Oo, hoo, you can't give your sweet woman
   Everything she wants in one time.
   Well, boys, she get ramblin' in her brain, hmm,
   Some monkey man on her mind.

Kind Hearted Woman Blues

Words and Music by Robert Johnson

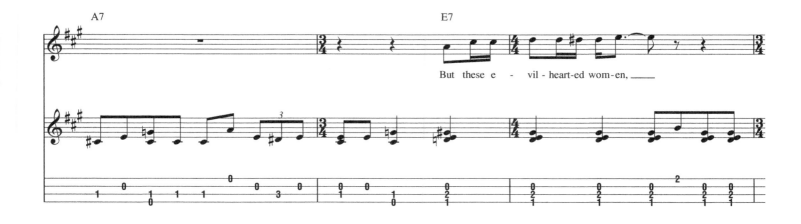

But these e - vil - heart-ed wom-en, _____

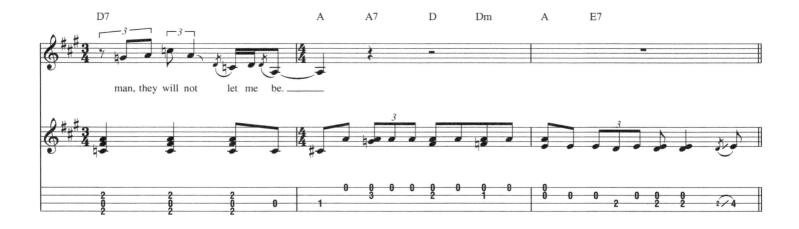

man, they will not let me be. _____

Verse

2. I love my ba-by, _____ my ba-by don't love _ me. _____

I love my ba-by, oo, _____ my _ ba-by don't _ love me. _____

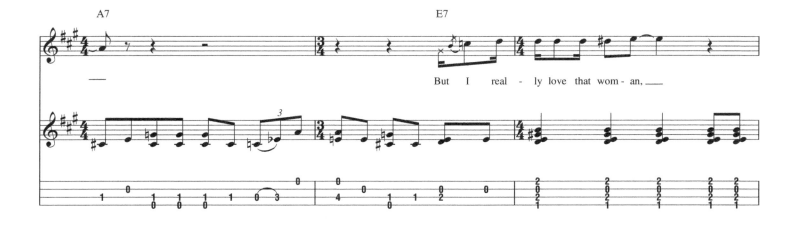

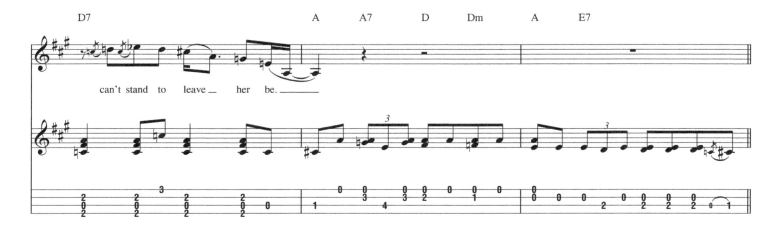

Bridge

You break ___ my heart ___ when you call ___

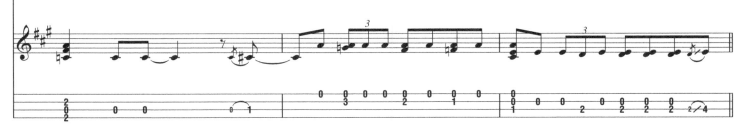

D7   A   A7   D   Dm   A   E7

___ Mis-ter So - and-So's name. ___

Solo

A7

D7

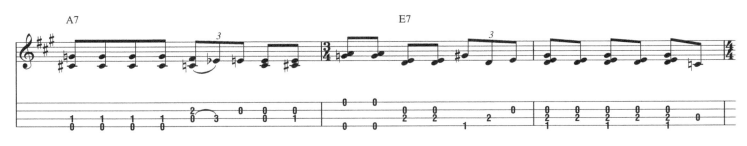

A7   E7

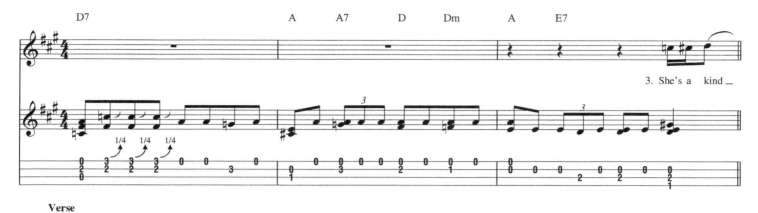

Verse

_____ heart-ed wom-an, _____ she stud-ies e - vil all the time. _____

She's a kind _____ heart - ed wom-an, _____ she stud-ies e - vil all the time.

You well's to kill me,

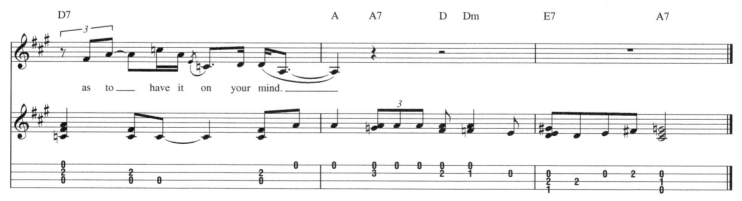

as to _____ have it on your mind. _____

Me and the Devil Blues

Words and Music by Robert Johnson

*Chord symbols reflect basic harmony.

I be-lieve it's time____ to go."

End Rhy. Fig. 1

Verse

2. Me and the Dev-il was walk-in' side____ by side.____

Rhy. Fig. 2

Me and the Dev-il, woo,_____ was walk-in' side____ by side.____

End Rhy. Fig. 2

And I'm go-in' to beat my wom-an____

Little Queen of Spades

Words and Music by Robert Johnson

*Chord symbols reflect basic harmony.

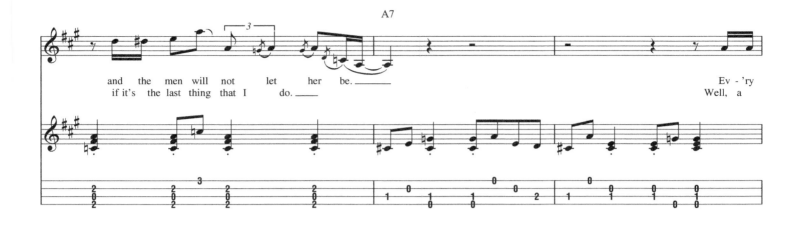

and the men will not let her be. ____
if it's the last thing that I do. ____
Ev - 'ry
Well, a

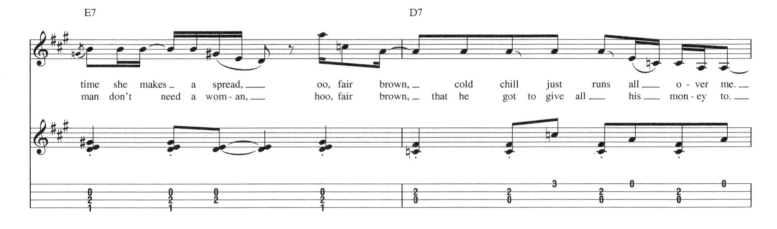

time she makes __ a spread, ____ oo, fair brown, __ cold chill just runs all __ o - ver me. ____
man don't need a wom - an, ____ hoo, fair brown, __ that he got to give all ____ his ____ mon - ey to. ____

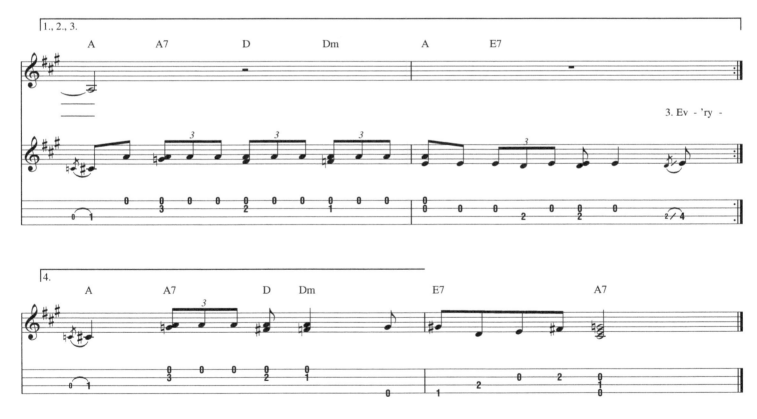

1., 2., 3.

A   A7   D   Dm   A   E7

3. Ev - 'ry -

4.

A   A7   D   Dm   E7   A7

Additional Lyrics

3. Ev'rybody say she got a mojo,
   Now she's been usin' that stuff.
   Mm, ev'rybody say she got a mojo
   'Cause she been usin' that stuff.
   But she got a way trimmin' down,
   Hoo, fair brown, and I mean it's most too tough.

4. Now, little girl, since I am the king,
   Baby, and you is the queen.
   Oo, hoo, since I am the king,
   Baby, and you is the queen.
   Let's us put our heads together,
   Hoo, fair brown, then we can make our money green.

Love in Vain Blues

Words and Music by Robert Johnson

*Chord symbols reflect basic harmony.

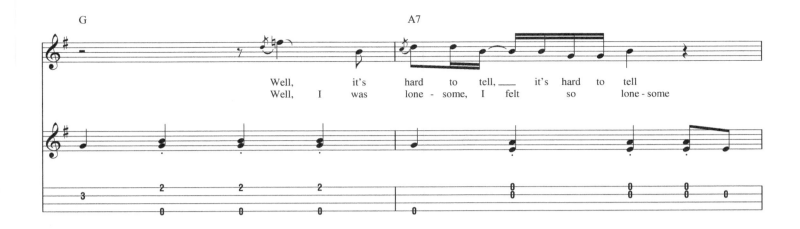

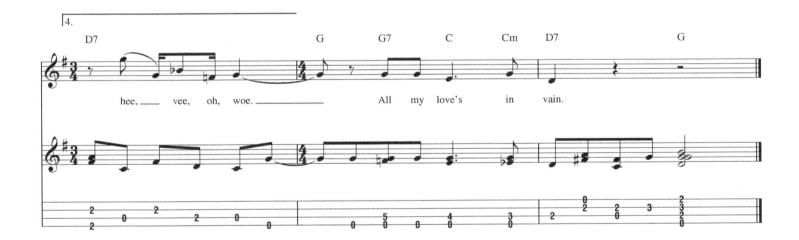

Additional Lyrics

3. When the train, it left the station
   With two lights on behind.
   When the train, it left the station
   With two lights on behind.
   Well, the blue light was my blues,
   And the red light was my mind.
   All my love's in vain.

4. Oo, hoo, hoo, Willie Mae.
   Oh, oh, hey, hoo, Willie Mae.
   Oo, oo, oo, oo, hee, vee, oh, woe.
   All my love's in vain.

Malted Milk

Words and Music by Robert Johnson

flow - ers is in May. _____ 2. Malt - ed

Verse

milk, malt - ed milk, _____ keep rush-in' to my head. _____ Malt -

Rhy. Fig. 1

ed milk, malt - ed milk, keep rush - in' to my head. _____

End Rhy. Fig. 1

And I have a fun - ny, fun - ny feel - ing _____ and I'm

knob keeps on turn - in', it must be spooks a - round my bed.

My door - knob keeps on turn - in', must be spooks a - round my bed.

I have a warm

old feel - in' and the hair ris - in' on my head.

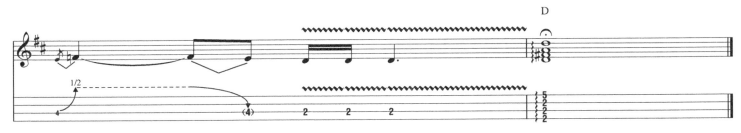

Phonograph Blues

Words and Music by Robert Johnson

- vil have I done? ____ What e - vil has the poor girl heard? ____

Verse

2. Bea - trice, I love my pho - no - graph, ____

End Rhy. Fig. 1

but you have broke my wind - in' chain. Bea - trice, I

w/ Rhy. Fig. 1

love my pho - no - gra', oo. Hon - ey, I broke my wind - in' chain. ____

And you've tak - en my lov - in' ____ and

give it to your oth - er man. ____ 3. Now, we

Verse

played it on ____ the so-fa, now. We played it 'side ____ the wall. My

nee-dles have got rust-y, ba-by, they will not play at all. ____ We played it on the

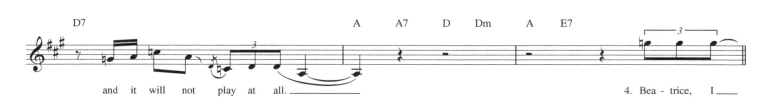

so - fa, _____ and we played it 'side ____ the wall.

But my nee-dles have got rust-y

and it will not play at all. _____ 4. Bea - trice, I ____

Verse

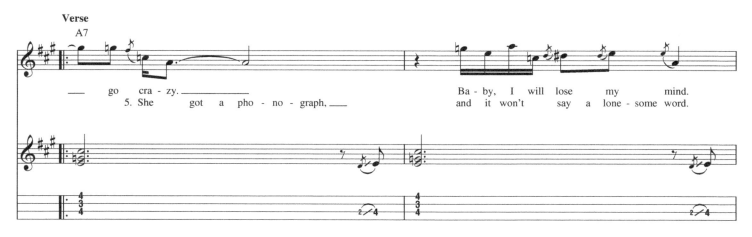

____ go cra - zy. _____

5. She got a pho - no - graph, ____ Ba - by, I will lose my mind.

and it won't say a lone - some word.

Stones in My Passway

Words and Music by Robert Johnson

*Chord symbols reflect basic harmony.

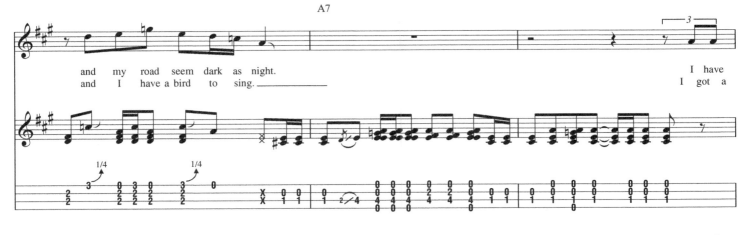

and my road seem dark as night.
and I have a bird to sing.

I have
I got a

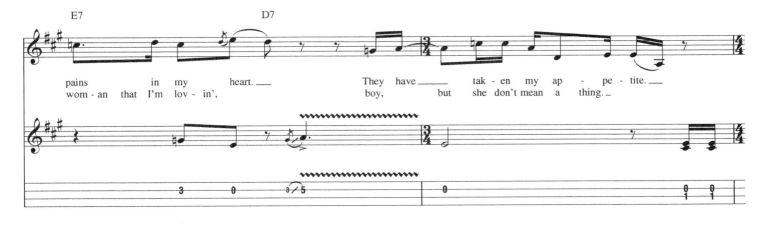

To Coda

pains in my heart.
wom-an that I'm lov-in',

They have
boy,

tak-en my ap-pe-tite.
but she don't mean a thing.

1., 2.
3.

2. I have a
3. My en-e-mies

Now you try'n' to

End Rhy. Fig. 1

Bridge

A7

take my life
and all my lov-in', too.

D.S. al Coda

Coda

Additional Lyrics

3. My enemies have betrayed me,
   Have overtaken poor Bob at last.
   My enemies have betrayed me,
   Have overtaken poor Bob at last.
   And there's one thing certainly,
   They have stones all in my pass.

4. I got three legs to truck home.
   Boys, please don't block my road.
   I got three legs to truck home.
   Boys, please don't block my road.
   I've been feelin' ashamed 'bout my rider.
   Babe, I'm booked and I got to go.

Sweet Home Chicago

Words and Music by Robert Johnson

*Chord symbols reflect basic harmony.

Stop Breakin' Down Blues

Words and Music by Robert Johnson

*Chord symbols reflect basic harmony.

Additional Lyrics

3. Now, you Saturday night womens,
You love to ape and clown.
You won't do nothin' but tear a
Good man reputation down.
Stop breakin' down.
Please, stop breakin' down.
The stuff I got'll bust your brains out, baby,
Hoo, it'll make you lose your mind.

4. Now, I give my baby, now,
The ninety-nine degree.
She jumped up and throwed a pistol down on me.
Stop breakin' down.
Please, stop breakin' down.
Stuff I got'll bust your brains out, baby,
Hoo, it'll make you lose your mind.

5. I can't start walkin' down the streets.
But some pretty mama don't start
Breakin' down with me.
Stop breakin' down.
Yes, stop breakin' down.
The stuff I got'll bust your brains out, baby,
Hoo, it'll make you lose your mind.

They're Red Hot

Words and Music by Robert Johnson

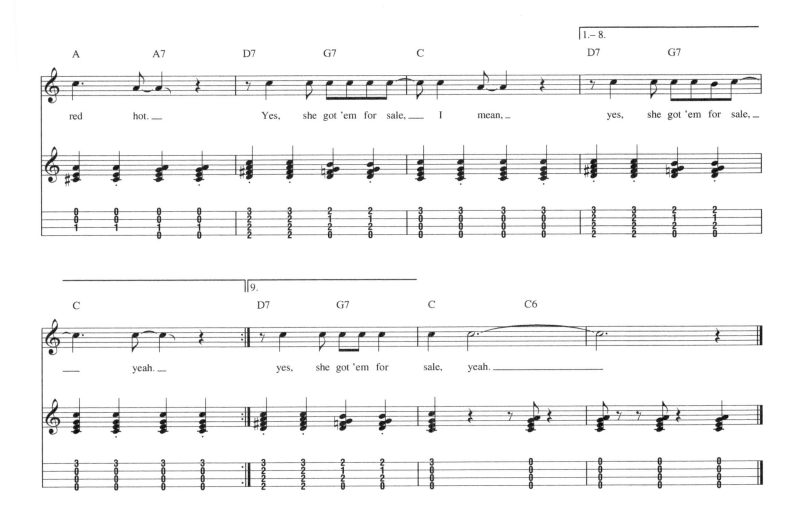

Additional Lyrics

3. Hot tamales and they're red hot.
Yes, she got 'em for sale.
Hot tamales and they're red hot.
Yes, she got 'em for sale.
I got a letter from a girl in the room,
Now she got somethin' good,
She got to bring home soon, now.
It's hot tamales and they're red hot.
Yes, she got 'em for sale.
I mean, yes, she got 'em for sale, yeah.

4. Hot tamales and they're red hot.
Yes, she got 'em for sale.
Hot tamales and they're red hot.
Yes, she got 'em for sale. *They're too hot, boy!*
The billy goat back in a bumble bee nest.
Ever since that, he can't take his rest, yeah.
Hot tamales and they're red hot.
Yeah, you got 'em for sale.
I mean, yes, she got 'em for sale, yeah.

5. Hot tamales and they're red hot.
Yes, she got 'em for sale.
Man, don't mess around 'em hot tamales, now,
'Cause they too black bad.
If you mess around 'em hot tamales
I'm 'onna upset your backbone,
Put your kidneys to sleep.
I'll due to break 'way your liver
And dare your heart to beat 'bout my
Hot tamales 'cause they're red hot.
Yes, she got 'em for sale.
I mean, yes, she got 'em for sale, yeah.

6. Hot tamales and they're red hot.
Yes, she got 'em for sale.
Hot tamales and they're red hot.
Yes, she got 'em for sale.
You know grandma laughs, and now grandpa, too.
Well, I wonder what in the world
We chillun gon' do, now.
Hot tamales and they're red hot.
Yes, she got 'em for sale.
I mean, yes, she got 'em for sale, yeah.

7. Hot tamales and they're red hot.
Yes, she got 'em for sale.
Hot tamales and they're red hot.
Yes, she got 'em for sale.
Me and my babe bought a V-8 Ford.
Well, we wind that thing all on the runnin' board, yes.
Hot tamales and they're red hot.
Yes, she got 'em for sale.
I mean, yes, she got 'em for sale, yeah.

8. Hot tamales and they're red hot.
Yes, she got 'em for sale. *They're too hot, boy!*
Hot tamales and they're red hot.
Yes, now, she got 'em for sale.
You know the monkey, now the baboon
Playin' in the grass.
Well, the monkey stuck his finger
In that good gulf gas, now.
Hot tamales and they're red hot.
Yes, she got 'em for sale.
I mean, yes, she got 'em for sale, yeah.

9. Hot tamales and they're red hot.
Yes, she got 'em for sale.
Hot tamales and they're red hot.
Yes, she got 'em for sale.
I got a girl, said she long and tall, now.
She sleeps in the kitchen with her feets in the hall, yes.
Hot tamales and they're red hot.
Yes, now, she got 'em for sale.
I mean, yes, she got 'em for sale, yeah.

32-20 Blues

Words and Music by Robert Johnson

*Chord symbols reflect basic harmony.

Verse

1. I send____ for my ba - by   and she don't come.____

I send____ for my ba - by,   man, and she don't

come._____   All the doc - tors in Hot__ Springs

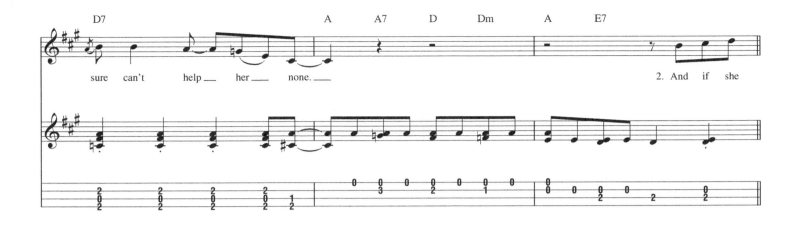

sure can't help ___ her ___ none. ___

2. And if she

Verse

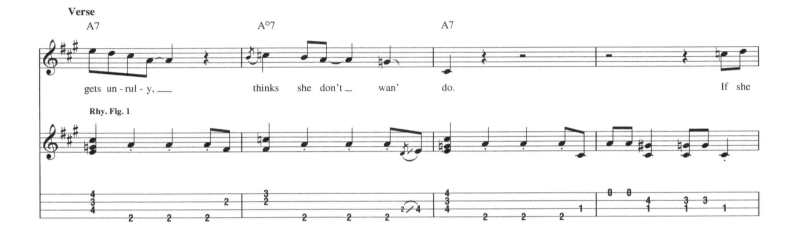

gets un-rul-y, ___ thinks she don't ___ wan' do.

If she

gets un-rul-y and thinks she don't ___ wan' do.

Take my

thir-ty two twen-ty, now, and cut her half ___ in ___ two. ___

3. She got a

End Rhy. Fig. 1

Verse

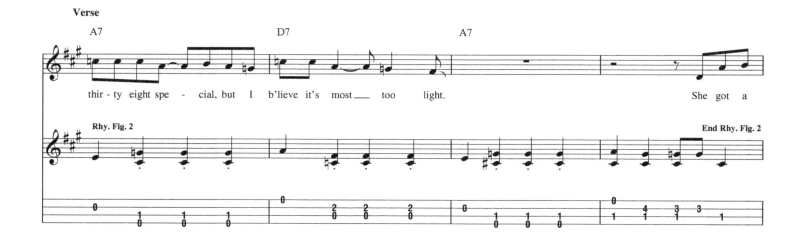

thir - ty eight spe - cial, but I b'lieve it's most ___ too light. She got a

thir - ty eight spe - cial, but I b'lieve it's most ___ too light.

I got a thir - ty two twen - ty, got to

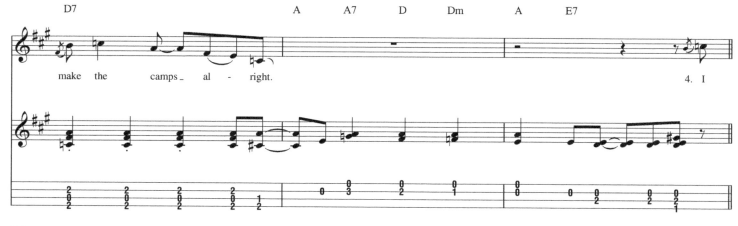

make the camps ___ al - right. 4. I

Verse

10. Ah, boys, I just can't take my rest. ___

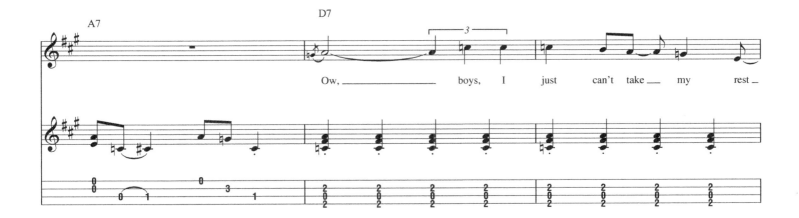

Ow, ___ boys, I just can't take ___ my rest ___

with this thir - ty two twen - ty lay - in'

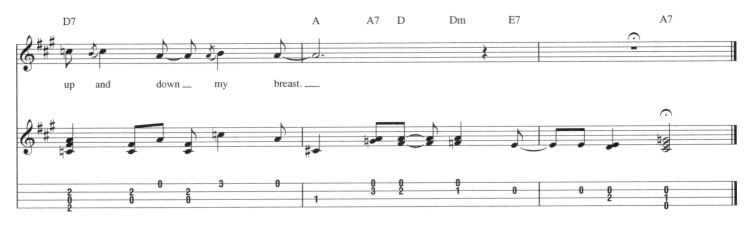

up and down ___ my breast. ___

When You Got a Good Friend

Words and Music by Robert Johnson

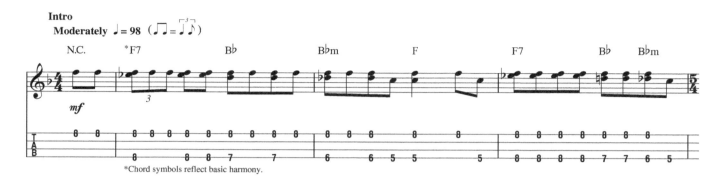

*Chord symbols reflect basic harmony.

1. When you got a good friend ____ that will stay right by ____

____ your side, ____ when you got a good friend ____

that will stay right by your side, ____

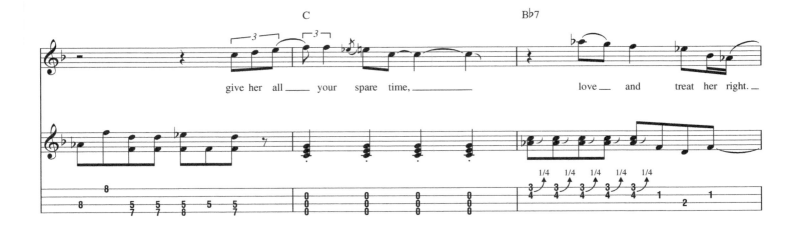

give her all ___ your spare time, _____ love ___ and treat her right.

2. I mis -

Verse

treat - ed my ba - by _____ and I can't see no rea-son why. _____
could I bear a - pol - o - gize, or would she __ sym - pa - thize with me? _____
babe, I may be right ay wrong. _____

Rhy. Fig. 1

I mis - treat - ed my ba - by, but I can't see no rea-son why. ___
Mm, _____ would she __ sym - pa - thize with me? ___
Ba-by, it's yo'y o - pin - ion, _____ oh, I may be right ay wrong.

UKULELE NOTATION LEGEND

THE MUSICAL STAFF shows pitches and rhythms and is divided by bar lines into measures. Pitches are named after the first seven letters of the alphabet.

TABLATURE graphically represents the ukulele fingerboard. Each horizontal line represents a a string, and each number represents a fret.

Notes:

Strings:

2nd string, 3rd fret   1st & 2nd strings open, played together   open F chord

HALF-STEP BEND: Strike the note and bend up 1/2 step.

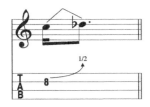

WHOLE-STEP BEND: Strike the note and bend up one step.

GRACE NOTE BEND: Strike the note and immediately bend up as indicated.

SLIGHT (MICROTONE) BEND: Strike the note and bend up 1/4 step.

BEND AND RELEASE: Strike the note and bend up as indicated, then release back to the original note. Only the first note is struck.

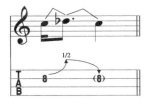

PRE-BEND: Bend the note as indicated, then strike it.

VIBRATO: The string is vibrated by rapidly bending and releasing the note with the fretting hand.

HAMMER-ON: Strike the first (lower) note with one finger, then sound the higher note (on the same string) with another finger by fretting it without picking.

PULL-OFF: Place both fingers on the notes to be sounded. Strike the first note and without picking, pull the finger off to sound the second (lower) note.

LEGATO SLIDE: Strike the first note and then slide the same fret-hand finger up or down to the second note. The second note is not struck.

SHIFT SLIDE: Same as legato slide, except the second note is struck.

TRILL: Very rapidly alternate between the notes indicated by continuously hammering on and pulling off.

TREMOLO PICKING: The note is picked as rapidly and continuously as possible.

NOTE: Tablature numbers in parentheses mean:

1. The note is being sustained over a system (note in standard notation is tied), or

2. The note is sustained, but a new articulation (such as a hammer-on, pull-off, slide or vibrato) begins, or

3. The note is a barely audible "ghost" note (note in standard notation is also in parentheses).

Additional Musical Definitions

(accent)	•	Accentuate note (play it louder)
(staccato)	•	Play the note short
D.S. al Coda	•	Go back to the sign (𝄋), then play until the measure marked "*To Coda*," then skip to the section labelled "Coda."
D.C. al Fine	•	Go back to the beginning of the song and play until the measure marked "*Fine*" (end).
N.C.	•	No chord.

• Repeat measures between signs.

• When a repeated section has different endings, play the first ending only the first time and the second ending only the second time.

The Best Collections for Ukulele

The Best Songs Ever

70 songs have now been arranged for ukulele. Includes: Always • Bohemian Rhapsody • Memory • My Favorite Things • Over the Rainbow • Piano Man • What a Wonderful World • Yesterday • You Raise Me Up • and more.

00282413 . . . . $17.99

Campfire Songs for Ukulele

30 favorites to sing as you roast marshmallows and strum your uke around the campfire. Includes: God Bless the U.S.A. • Hallelujah • The House of the Rising Sun • I Walk the Line • Puff the Magic Dragon • Wagon Wheel • You Are My Sunshine • and more.

00129170 . . . . $14.99

The Daily Ukulele

arr. Liz and Jim Beloff
Strum a different song everyday with easy arrangements of 365 of your favorite songs in one big songbook! Includes favorites by the Beatles, Beach Boys, and Bob Dylan, folk songs, pop songs, kids' songs, Christmas carols, and Broadway and Hollywood tunes, all with a spiral binding for ease of use.

00240356 Original Edition $39.99
00240681 Leap Year Edition $39.99
00119270 Portable Edition $37.50

Disney Hits for Ukulele

Play 23 of your favorite Disney songs on your ukulele. Includes: The Bare Necessities • Cruella De Vil • Do You Want to Build a Snowman? • Kiss the Girl • Lava • Let It Go • Once upon a Dream • A Whole New World • and more.

00151250 . . . . $16.99

Also available:

00291547 **Disney Fun Songs for Ukulele** . . . $16.99
00701708 **Disney Songs for Ukulele** $14.99
00334696 **First 50 Disney Songs on Ukulele** . $16.99

First 50 Songs You Should Play on Ukulele

An amazing collec-tion of 50 accessible, must-know favorites: Edelweiss • Hey, Soul Sister • I Walk the Line • I'm Yours • Imagine • Over the Rainbow • Peaceful Easy Feeling • The Rainbow Connection • Riptide • more.

00149250 . . . . $16.99

Also available:

00292082 **First 50 Melodies on Ukulele** . . . $15.99
00289029 **First 50 Songs on Solo Ukulele** . . $15.99
00347437 **First 50 Songs to Strum on Uke** . $16.99

40 Most Streamed Songs for Ukulele

40 top hits that sound great on uke! Includes: Despacito • Feel It Still • Girls like You • Happier • Havana • High Hopes • The Middle • Perfect • 7 Rings • Shallow • Shape of You • Something Just like This • Stay • Sucker • Sunflower • Sweet but Psycho • Thank U, Next • There's Nothing Holdin' Me Back • Without Me • and more!

00298113 . . . . $17.99

The 4 Chord Songbook

With just 4 chords, you can play 50 hot songs on your ukulele! Songs include: Brown Eyed Girl • Do Wah Diddy Diddy • Hey Ya! • Ho Hey • Jessie's Girl • Let It Be • One Love • Stand by Me • Toes • With or Without You • and many more.

00142050 . . . . $16.99

Also available:

00141143 **The 3-Chord Songbook** $16.99

Pop Songs for Kids

30 easy pop favorites for kids to play on uke, including: Brave • Can't Stop the Feeling! • Feel It Still • Fight Song • Happy • Havana • House of Gold • How Far I'll Go • Let It Go • Remember Me (Ernesto de la Cruz) • Rewrite the Stars • Roar • Shake It Off • Story of My Life • What Makes You Beautiful • and more.

00284415 . . . . $16.99

Simple Songs for Ukulele

50 favorites for standard G-C-E-A ukulele tuning, including: All Along the Watchtower • Can't Help Falling in Love • Don't Worry, Be Happy • Ho Hey • I'm Yours • King of the Road • Sweet Home Alabama • You Are My Sunshine • and more.

00156815 . . . . $14.99

Also available:

00276644 **More Simple Songs for Ukulele** . $14.99

Top Hits of 2020

18 uke-friendly tunes of 2020 are featured in this collection of melody, lyric and chord arrangements in standard G-C-E-A tuning. Includes: Adore You (Harry Styles) • Before You Go (Lewis Capaldi) • Cardigan (Taylor Swift) • Daisies (Katy Perry) • I Dare You (Kelly Clarkson) • Level of Concern (twenty one pilots) • No Time to Die (Billie Eilish) • Rain on Me (Lady Gaga feat. Ariana Grande) • Say So (Doja Cat) • and more.

00355553 . . . . $14.99

Also available:

00302274 **Top Hits of 2019** $14.99

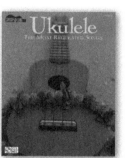

Ukulele: The Most Requested Songs

Strum & Sing Series
Cherry Lane Music
Nearly 50 favorites all expertly arranged for ukulele! Includes: Bubbly • Build Me Up, Buttercup • Cecilia • Georgia on My Mind • Kokomo • L-O-V-E • Your Body Is a Wonderland • and more.

02501453 . . . . $14.99

The Ultimate Ukulele Fake Book

Uke enthusiasts will love this giant, spiral-bound collection of over 400 songs for uke! Includes: Crazy • Dancing Queen • Downtown • Fields of Gold • Happy • Hey Jude • 7 Years • Summertime • Thinking Out Loud • Thriller • Wagon Wheel • and more.

00175500 9" x 12" Edition $45.00
00319997 5.5" x 8.5" Edition $39.99

Learn to play the
Ukulele
with these great Hal Leonard books!

Hal Leonard Ukulele Method

Book 1
by Lil' Rev

The *Hal Leonard Ukulele Method* is designed for anyone just learning to play ukulele. This comprehensive and easy-to-use beginner's guide by acclaimed performer and uke master Lil' Rev includes many fun songs of different styles to learn and play. The accompanying audio contains 46 tracks of songs for demonstration and play along. Includes: types of ukuleles, tuning, music reading, melody playing, chords, strumming, scales, tremolo, music notation and tablature, a variety of music styles, ukulele history and much more.

00695847 Book Only	$6.99
00695832 Book/Online Audio	$10.99
00320534 DVD	$14.95

Book 2
00695948 Book Only	$6.99
00695949 Book/Online Audio	$10.99

Ukulele Chord Finder
00695803 9" x 12"	$7.99
00695902 6" x 9"	$6.99
00696472 Book 1 with Online Audio + Chord Finder	$15.99

Ukulele Scale Finder
00696378 9" x 12"	$6.99

Easy Songs for Ukulele
00695904 Book/Online Audio	$14.99
00695905 Book	$7.99

Ukulele for Kids
00696468 Book/Online Audio	$12.99
00244855 Method & Songbook	$19.99

Baritone Ukulele Method – Book 1
00696564 Book/Online Audio	$10.99

Jake Shimabukuro Teaches Ukulele Lessons

Learn notes, chords, songs, and playing techniques from the master of modern ukulele! In this unique book with online video, Jake Shimabukuro will get you started on playing the ukulele. The book includes full transcriptions of every example, the video features Jake teaching you everything you need to know plus video of Jake playing all the examples.

00320992 Book/Online Video $19.99

Ukulele Aerobics
For All Levels, from Beginner to Advanced
by Chad Johnson

This package provides practice material for every day of the week and includes an online audio access code for all the workouts in the book. Techniques covered include: strumming, fingerstyle, slides, bending, damping, vibrato, tremolo and more.

00102162 Book/Online Audio $19.99

Fretboard Roadmaps – Ukulele
The Essential Patterns That All the Pros Know and Use
by Fred Sokolow & Jim Beloff

Take your uke playing to the next level! Tunes and exercises in standard notation and tab illustrate each technique. Absolute beginners can follow the diagrams and instruction step-by-step, while intermediate and advanced players can use the chapters non-sequentially to increase their understanding of the ukulele. The audio includes 59 demo and play-along tracks.

00695901 Book/Online Audio $14.99

All About Ukulele
A Fun and Simple Guide to Playing Ukulele
by Chad Johnson

If you wish there was a fun and engaging way to motivate you in your uke playing quest, then this is it: All About Ukulele is for you. Whether it's learning to read music, playing in a band, finding the right instrument, or all of the above, this enjoyable guide will help you.

00233655 Book/Online Audio $19.99

Play Ukulele Today!
A Complete Guide to the Basics
by Barrett Tagliarino

This is the ultimate self-teaching method for ukulele! Includes audio with full demo tracks and over 60 great songs. You'll learn: care for the instrument; how to produce sound; reading music notation and rhythms; and more.

00699638 Book/Online Audio	$10.99
00293927 Book 1 & 2/Online Media	$19.99

HAL•LEONARD®
www.halleonard.com

HAL·LEONARD® UKULELE PLAY-ALONG

Now you can play your favorite songs on your uke with great-sounding backing tracks to help you sound like a bona fide pro! The audio also features playback tools so you can adjust the tempo without changing the pitch and loop challenging parts.

HAL·LEONARD®

www.halleonard.com

Prices, contents, and availability subject to change without notice.